Days with the Universal Mother Volume 2

tava kathāmṛtaṁ tapta jīvanam
kavibhirīḍitaṁ kalmaṣapaham
śravaṇamaṅgalaṁ śrīmatātataṁ
bhuvi gṛṇanti te bhurida janaḥ

The nectar of your excellences revives the scorched spirit of mankind.
It purifies the sinner while holy men live on it.
To hear it is itself auspicious and peace generating.
They are the real gift makers who spread your name far and wide.

Śrīmad Bhāgavatam 10.31.9

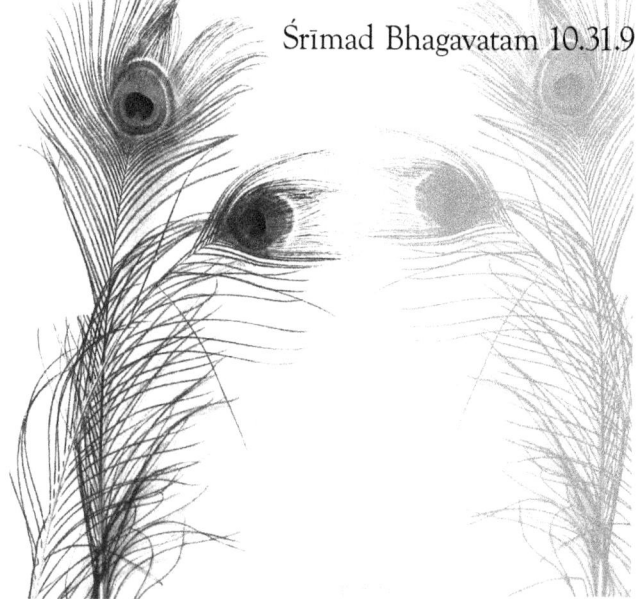

Days with the Universal Mother

Volume Two

Swamini Atmaprana

**Days with the Universal Mother
Volume 2**
Swamini Atmaprana

Published by:
 Mata Amritanandamayi Center
 P.O. Box 613
 San Ramon, CA 94583-0613 USA
 USA

First edition: April 2019

Copyright © 2019 by Mata Amritanandamayi Center, P.O. Box 613, San Ramon, CA 94583, United States

All rights reserved. No part of this publication may be stored in a retrieval system, transmitted, reproduced, transcribed or translated into any language, in any form, by any means without the prior agreement and written permission of the publisher.

In India:
 www.amritapuri.org
 inform@amritapuri.org

In USA:
 amma.org

In Europe:
 www.amma-europe.org

Contents

Dedication	7
Tasmai Śrī Gurave Namaḥ	9
Amma – The Personification of Patience	17
Oṁ Śiva-Śaktyaikya Rūpiṇyai Namaḥ	25
Amma – The Sum Total of Divine Energy	37
Oṁ Nāma Pārāyaṇa Prītāyai Namaḥ	51
Mṛtyor mā Amṛtaṁ Gamaya	67
Amma – The Inner Guide	87

Dedication

oṁ paramātma svarūpiṇīṁ
mātṛ rūpa manoharīṁ
amṛtānandamayīṁ tvāṁ
pranamāmi muhurmuhuḥ

O, my Divine Mother, the reality of all that exists, the mother of the whole world who attracts all beings with love and makes everyone happy, let me prostrate at your lotus feet again and again.

With humble prostrations I offer this book at my Guru's holy feet, and my thanks to all the friends who have given their invaluable service in preparing it.

lokāḥ samastāḥ sukhino bhavantu

May the whole world attain everlasting peace and happiness.

In Service to Amma,
Atmaprana
April 2018, Amritapuri

Om Amṛteśwaryai Namaḥ

Chapter 1

Tasmai Śrī Gurave Namaḥ

ajñānatimirāndhasya jñānāñjanaśalākayā
cakṣurunmīlitaṁ yena tasmai śrī gurave namaḥ

I prostrate at the sacred feet of Amma, the supreme spiritual teacher, who reveals Her true nature to Her disciples by applying the collyrium of knowledge, thus removing the cataract of ignorance from their blinded eyes.

The tradition of Bhārata (India) includes the successive advent of *satgurus* (realized spiritual teachers). It was sage Vyasa who divided the Vedas into Ṛk, Yajus, Sāma, and Atharva and taught them to his four disciples. Hence his birthday is celebrated as Guru's Day on the full moon day in July (*Guru Purṇima*). In the present day, Amma, the greatest among Gurus, imparts spiritual knowledge even while engaging herself in various activities. Amma aims to expand the spiritual and mundane views of her disciples. In the initial period of the ashram, Amma graciously volunteered to take up any work that came her way for the growth of the ashram and the ashramites, be it carrying sand, construction work of the prayer hall or channeling the rainwater from the courtyard to prepare the ashram premises for the birthday celebrations.

One day while doing sand seva with Amma, I found the shovel too heavy for me and slid the sand into the carry-bag with my hands. Observing that, Amma made fun of me, calling me *annarakannan*, the squirrel. I felt blessed to hear that merciful address of Amma, remembering the story of the squirrel in connection with the life of Śrī Rāma. Bhagavān Śrī Rāma, Lakṣmaṇa, and the monkey-soldiers such as Hanumān, Sugrīva and the others, were building the bridge connecting Sri Lanka with Ramesvaram. Strong monkeys were bringing big trees and rocks for the bridge, while the small squirrel rolled in the mud and went into the sea to deposit the sand covering its body for the bridge. Śrī Rāma was very pleased to see the squirrel's persevering efforts. He took it in his hand and lovingly stroked its back with his three fingers. It is said that three lines appeared on its back, which remain even today. The proverb "The squirrel also does what it can" has become very popular in the Malayalam language.

Sometimes Amma removes the accumulated negative tendencies of her disciples by making them do physical work. These tendencies might be the result of wrong thoughts, words or deeds committed in the past. Once, when we were taking part in the construction work of the prayer hall with Amma, she made me carry the sand for mixing the concrete for three days. As a result my weak back became very stiff. On the following day I travelled with Amma to Palakkad, a city in northern Kerala. At that time there was no branch of M.A. Math there; Amma's programmes were conducted in public auditoriums. After Amma's divine programmes, we came back to the ashram on a bhāva darśan day. As usual, I sat erect in meditation in Amma's divine presence in the kalari (old temple) during the bhāva darśan. Afterwards, though my mind was calm and composed, I suffered from unbearable back pain. I was in bed for some days, and later on I was cured by Amma. It was clear to me that Amma was deliberately taking away the accumulated tendencies in me.

In those days, when Amma used to sit outside in the yard under the starlit sky after the evening bhajans, I often got some time with her as her personal attendant. One evening, most unexpectedly, Amma proceeded towards the brahmacharinis' residential area and started to clean a clogged drain that was overflowing and stinking. Seeing Amma there, a few brahmacharis came running and joined in the work, but kept a safe distance so as not to make their clothes dirty. When Amma saw that the work was not progressing She Herself stepped into the drain and started to remove the accumulated sludge with her own hands. Then the brahmacharis also followed her and shoveled the filth out of it. After the work was over Amma came out with her holy feet black with dirt. All those who were present competed to bring water and wash Amma's feet. She told them "Amma does not expect any of you to wash her feet; you have to see the entire ashram area as Amma's feet and keep it clean always". It was as if Amma, the Universal Mother, was proclaiming the Vedic mantra that the origin of the earth is from the feet of "virat purusha[1]". Amma also taught the ashramites how to handle the disposal of sewage from the septic tank connected to the ashram toilets. The training they received from Amma enabled them later on to take up such projects as cleaning pilgrim centers like Shabarimala and the Amala Bharatam project.

I put the direct and indirect lessons that I received from Amma into practice while I was doing public service in the Thrissur branch of the M. A. Math. At that time, even the construction of the ground floor of the ashram building there had not been finished completely. During monsoon, water that came in from the courtyard and the roof, flooded the floor. Yet, with temporary arrangements we could organize the monthly retreat and similar programmes. We also planned to conduct the Guru Purnima programmes there, with necessary adjustments to combat heavy rainfall.

---

[1] Purusha sooktam, Rig veda 10, 96

Continuous chanting of the Lalita Sahasranama and distribution of clothes, books and medicines for financially disadvantaged students were carried out on a daily basis during the entire month. Devotees extended their physical and financial support for preparing the interior and exterior of the hall for the ensuing celebrations. By Amma's grace, new devotees came and joined the work. It was during the same year that a member of the Kerala Legislative Assembly made a sacrilegious statement about Amma[2]. Almost all of the ashram centers in Kerala organized processions and meetings in protest. I published an article in one of the daily newspapers in which I mentioned that the flames of protest of the devotees would rise high on Guru Purnima.

On the day of Guru Purnima, the celebrations started in the morning with the chanting of hymns and the 'Guru paduka puja' and was followed by soul-stirring devotional singing. Thousands of devotees joined the worship mentally. The devotees were taking a short rest after lunch when suddenly the whole atmosphere became clouded and dark as if night had set in. To avoid

---

[2] Later, he had to confess his mistake and apologize to Amma.

the impending rain, we had to prepare the starting of the procession (shobhayatra) before beginning the afternoon programmes, contrary to what was announced previously. Ashramites led the procession in which hundreds of devotees participated. Leading the procession in front was an open vehicle with girls wearing the costumes of Amma, and Durga, Lakshmi, and Saraswati – the three aspects of Amma, which gave a visual treat to the public. The song-

*"Durgā Lakṣmī, Saraswatī Devi Jaganmātā,
Devi Jaganmātā Mātā Amṛtānandamayī"*

and other bhajans were sung with great fervour. After raising slogans in front of the city station, the devotees returned to the ashram for the evening programme. The famous Malayalam poet and close devotee of Amma, the late Sri Kunjunni, presided over the public meeting. The esteemed presidential address and the informative speeches of well-wishers and devotees kept the audience spellbound. With my valedictory address, and the evening bhajans we concluded the entire festival before sunset. Both the audience and organisers noted that in no way did the rain disturb any of the programmes. I had noticed that, by Amma's grace, the atmosphere had become bright again during and after the procession. I was convinced that Amma was granting the prayer I had included in the printed circular, "May the Guru Purnima day become bright with a lively procession". Once more I experienced that Amma is omniscient and knows each word, thought and action of her disciples and guides them accordingly.

Oṁ Namaḥ Śivāya

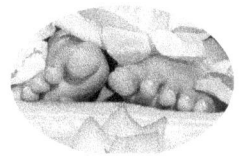

Oṁ Amṛteśwaryai Namaḥ

Chapter 2

Amma – The Personification of Patience

During the initial days of the ashram, Amma - the Universal Mother, expressed her divinity mainly through activities like training the ashramites spiritually, giving Bhava darshan (Amma appearing to the devotees in the form of Sri Krishna and the Divine Mother), and conducting spiritual programmes in several parts of Kerala. Amma, being the absolute existence-knowledge-bliss - Poorna brahma swarupini - had nothing to achieve, for there was nothing beyond her reach. Yet She was continuously engaged in activities meant for the good of the entire world, thus setting an example for Her children to follow. In those days, the ashram was completely isolated from the world outside and there were no modern facilities, not even a telephone to disturb the silence of the ashram. It was usual for the brahmacharis and brahmacharinis to meditate near the backwater ponds in which the coconut trees with their fronds swaying and singing "Amma, Amma" and dancing in the bright morning light cast their reflection. The gentle breeze created a flutter of little waves moving the water in the ponds and splitting the images of the coconut trees, giving a transient mistaken impression that the trees themselves were split into pieces. This apparent reflection reminded me of the indwelling self in the form of Amma who remains unchanged, even while changes like old age, disease and death affect the body. One morning while I was meditating, a thought cropped up in my mind, "The drama of the divine play of all the previous incarnations is being enacted in Amma's life now". Very soon I heard Amma loudly scolding someone in the ashram, and later on I came to know that She was punishing a brahmachari for some reason.

Amma — The Personification of Patience

That day in the evening Amma travelled with the ashramites for a programme in another ashram. She appeared to regret the severe punishment She had given to Her son. As if to forget the whole thing, Amma took little Sivan in Her lap and caressed him and made him meditate for a few moments. The venue of the function was the Vijayananda Ashram at Kitangannur in Alappuzha district. After the grand reception given to Amma, Her divine singing commenced and the soul stirring bhajans threw the audience into a rapture. When the bhajans were over Amma started to give darshan to the thousands of people gathered there. She received them one by one, consoling them, wiping their tears and solving their problems. Finally, with a warm hug She gave each one some prasad. After the programme concluded, the residents of the ashram approached Amma and expressed their desire to host Her and Her children at their ashram at night. Amma agreed to their proposal and blessed them. It was late in the night when Amma rested for a while. I sat near Her massaging Her holy feet while She conversed with me about the programme. Amma suddenly asked me, "How was the play today?" On hearing Her words I sat spellbound and remembered my thought about Amma's eternal play. I felt blessed and was once again convinced that Amma is Sarvajna, the all-knowing indwelling self in every being. I prostrated at Her lotus feet mentally again and again and continued to offer my service.

On another occasion, we were traveling with Amma in the ashram van when two of the brahmacharis started to discuss the divine attributes of Sri Rama and Sri Krishna. The discussion went on for a long time and ended in a heated argument as to who is the greater of the two Incarnations. For a while Amma was taking part in it joining with both sides. Yet the discussion went on endlessly. Then She had to stop them with enlightening words, "My children, have you realized Sri Rama or Sri Krishna? If you have direct knowledge about them, you would be able to discuss with conviction. Until then, it is better to keep quiet and do sadhana." Then Amma pointed to the ripe rice field and continued, "Can you harvest these crops which belong to someone else? First you have to own the field and prepare it well and then sow the seeds. When the seedlings appear you must tend them carefully with water and necessary manure, and when they are fully grown you can with authority reap the harvest. Likewise, the seed of spirituality must grow and bear the fruit of realization, and then you can speak with authority." All of us imbibed Amma's apt advice which opened our inner eyes. I was reminded of one of Sri Shankara's teachings to his disciples, "Keep away from wrong argumentation, and always keep reflecting on the import of scriptural revelations." (Sadhana Panchakam, -3)

It was on the occasion of another 'reception programme' that Amma made us understand the importance of the great quality of patience. She was invited to a small temple somewhere in the interior of Alappuzha district. As usual, She accepted the invitation and reached the venue with the ashramites, but none of the people in the temple came forward to receive Her. Instead, some arrogant youngsters tried to insult Her, talking loudly and using abusive language. The brahmacharis could not tolerate this kind of rude behaviour on the part of the 'organizers' and were going to retort immediately. Amma stopped them and said, "This is not our way; we have to be patient and go back to the ashram. My children, it is not proper for us to quarrel with these people." Amma was not upset in the least and asked Her children to get into the van. Everyone obeyed Her and soon all of us reached Vallikavu (a village on the shore of the backwaters) and we stepped from the van into the pole boat. To our pleasant surprise we saw that many devotees were waiting to receive Amma on the other shore of the backwater near the ashram. We were surprised because in those days very few devotees came to the ashram for Amma's darshan on the non-Bhava darshan days. For Amma, the insult from the temple and the warm welcome from the ashram were alike. The ashramites understood that Amma had planned the whole incident in order to teach them the greatness of patience and the capacity to accept all situations with equanimity.

The scriptural texts like the Mahabharatam, Srimad Bhagavatam, etc., also teach the necessity of having patience. Yudhishthira, the eldest among the Pandavas, could save his life while he was in the forest with his wife and brothers only because he had the quality of patience. He was asked by a Yaksha, "Who is more perseverant than the earth?", to which he answered "mother". The Yaksha was pleased and allowed him to quench his thirst by drinking water from the pond owned by the Yaksha. Four of Yudhishthira's younger brothers had fallen dead because they were impatient with the Yaksha and did not wait to answer his questions.[3] The Srimad Bhagavatam (11,7, 37) mentions that the mendicant had 24 gurus; Mother earth who was one of them taught him the ideal of perseverance. The earth endures all that is done to it by human beings. Nowadays people even disfigure and pollute the face of the earth with waste materials like plastic. The plastic is a necessary evil of the modern age which even alters the composition and equilibrium of the earth. The earth is found to tolerate all the assaults, but for the rare reactions like earthquakes, tsunamis, etc. Amma's divine opinion is that these disasters are caused by the selfish actions of human beings. In the present age, Amma, the personification of patience and tolerance, has built institutions for promoting selfless humanitarian activities, and trains Her disciples for the same. From the early years of my ashram

---

[3] Yaksha prashnam, Mahabharatham

life Amma advised me to cultivate the attitude of a loving and persevering mother. If I became impatient either during the day-to-day ashram life or while interacting with the hospital patients, Amma immediately corrected me with Her benevolent intervention. Once while Amma was conversing with a devotee, She told him while pointing to me, "Leelamol must become pure like unalloyed gold; the strict disciplining is for her evolvement." With a heart full of gratitude and prayers for total surrender I bowed down again and again to Amma, the Supreme Teacher.

Oṁ Namaḥ Śivāya

Oṁ Amṛteśwaryai Namaḥ

Chapter 3

Oṁ Śiva-Śaktyaikya Rūpiṇyai Namaḥ[4]

Amma has installed Brahmasthanam temples in almost all Her ashram branches in India. Worship in these temples enables the devotees to experience unity in diversity[5]. She installed the first temple in Kodungallur, a town in central Kerala, where a famous age-old Devi temple was already in existence. The sanctity of Brahmasthanam

---

[4] Lalita Sahasranama Stotram mantra 999: Salutations to Her who is not different from the union of Shiva and Shakti, always equal and identical.

[5] These unique temples have a central four-sided stone with images of Devi, Ganesh, Shiva and Rahu carved on them.

temples is greater than in other places of worship, since Amma Herself installed them. They exude the divine vibrations of Amma, especially during the annual festivals. In the early years, the festival lasted for seven days. Daily programmes included Lalita Sahasranama archana (chanting of the thousand names of the Divine Mother with offering of flowers), spiritual discourses, Amma's darshan every evening and every night, evening bhajans and various cultural events put up by Her children. The public could solve many of their day-to-day problems doing pujas by themselves under the guidance of brahmacharis.

One evening, after public darshan, Amma was giving darshan in Her room to a few devotees. After everyone had left, a young man came for darshan and spoke to Amma apologetically. The problem came about in the following manner. This man, who was an artist in one of the popular monthly magazines for children, had published a series of picture stories in which he had been disrespectful to Amma. Following this incident, which pained the devotees, he had to face several calamities in his life. Very soon the publishers too had to close down their press. Yet he was not

Oṁ Śiva-Śaktyaikya Rūpiṇyai Namaḥ

---

ready to accept his mistake. Later on, following the series of mishaps, he became more thoughtful and receptive and was ready to correct himself. Praying mentally to Amma for forgiveness he planned to start a new monthly magazine for children. He had prepared the first copy and brought it to be blessed by Amma during the Brahmasthanam festival, and with the help of the organisers had come to Her room for darshan. He prostrated at Amma's feet and begged for forgiveness. Amma who is all-merciful, consoled him saying, "My son, Amma doesn't care for what others say about Her. But if the devotees who depend on me are pained, a negative vibration is seen to arise in nature, which will have an adverse effect on those responsible for it." Amma's consoling words and Her divine love were new experiences for the writer who later shared them with the audience while addressing them. He went back with a light heart after this episode.

One young devotee of Amma, a teacher at the Vivekananda Kendra School in Arunachal Pradesh, used to come for Amma's darshan during the Kodungallur festival. Her desire was to become a member of Amma's ashram, to which

Amma did not agree initially. Every year she returned to Arunachal Pradesh with a sorrowful heart. Later, for the sake of many such devotees, Amma founded Amrita Vidyalayams, the first of which was in Kotungallur. The young devotee, who had become a brahmacharini of the ashram, was appointed as the principal.

Once when Amma was about to leave the ashram for the Brahmasthanam festival in Kozhikode, She called me to Her room and gave me permission to accompany Her as Her personal attendant. While Amma was taking leave of a few of Her children who were staying back, I was putting together Her personal belongings, ready to be kept in Her car. Soon Amma got up to leave, and I followed Her blissfully and sat with Her in the car. Amma and I were in the backseat while the Swamis sat in the front. Amma was conversing with them regarding some ashram matters and I was totally focused on Amma to know whether She needed anything. Suddenly I felt that Amma needed Her face towel. I looked for the bag containing the necessities, but alas! I could not find it. Immediately I brought the matter to Amma's notice and She told the Swamis to

Oṁ Śiva-Śaktyaikya Rūpiṇyai Namaḥ

send word to the car behind. Soon Amma's bag was brought and the towel was handed over to Her. I was relieved to see that Amma used it as usual. I realised that She saved me because I was attentive and totally focused on Amma, the Ocean of Mercy. She was teaching me the importance of *sraddha* - one-pointed attention and faith in the Guru and saving me from critical situations that could have arisen during the journey.

Svalpamapyasya dharmasya
Trāyate mahato bhayāt (2:40)

"Even a little of this karma-yogic discipline delivers one from the peril of transmigratory life with its birth, death and so forth."

I remembered this verse from the Bhagavad Gita.

In those days, on the way to Kozhikode Amma used to swim and bathe in the holy river Bharata Puzha. That year too, Amma and Her children eagerly alighted from the vehicles and prepared for a swim. Then I could hand over Amma's clothes to Her, only because She had graciously reminded me of the bag in the car in the beginning of the journey. Otherwise I could have been in great trouble. Prostrating mentally at Amma's sacred feet, I accompanied Her to the river. Amma, the personification of Gayatri Devi, instructed us to take water in both hands, chant the Gayatri mantra, pour it into the river, and take a dip in the river, repeatedly. Amma made Her children realise that the Gayatri mantra[6] gives a taste of divine bliss and then spiritual enlightenment by establishing a strong bond between the Guru and Her disciples. After bathing, all of us sat on the vast sandy shore of the river and had lunch blessed by Amma. Thereafter, we sat around Amma and meditated in Her divine presence. The flowing holy river, the skyscraping blue mountains, trees and cooling breeze, made meditation easy. In the evening we continued the journey and reached the Kozhikode ashram. The devotees and the ashramites welcomed Amma with pada puja and prayers. As thousands of people took Amma's darshan daily during the festival, She got very little

---

[6] Oṁ bhūr bhuvaḥ svaḥ - Tat savitur vareṇyaṁ
Bhargo devasya dhīmahi - Dhiyo yo naḥ pracodayāt
We meditate on the effulgence of the Self-luminous Param-atman, who, as the indwelling Self in all beings, inspires our intellect.

Oṁ Śiva-Śaktyaikya Rūpiṇyai Namaḥ

rest. Amma also gave me an occasion to address the audience, and I was fortunate to serve Her to the best of my ability during the festival days.

Many years later, I got the opportunity to be closely involved in the festival activities in Kozhikode when Amma sent me there as head of the ashram branch. I composed and directed two dance dramas for the Amrita Vidyalayam students. In the first year of my stay there, I selected a hymn in Malayalam – "Bhagavad Gita Saram" (Gist of Bhagavad Gita). Though I composed the drama, giving music to the hymn, I could not find any talented singers nor someone who could record it. One day, a youth came to me as if sent by Amma Herself. He and his younger sister were good musicians and singers who had sung in Amma's presence regularly during the previous annual festivals. He had come to register their names for singing in the upcoming festival. One of the teachers at Amrita Vidyalayam, who was also involved in organising the extra-curricular activities of the school, happened to meet him by Amma's grace. Suhe brought him along and introduced him to me. I explained the concept and requirements of the dance-drama, and he was quick to grasp the format I had in mind. He sang beautifully and recorded some parts, and the remaining parts were sung by students and recorded at the ashram. After the grand performance on the festival stage, Amma encouraged and blessed all the participants by giving them a good darshan and prasad.

The following year, we dramatised the Divine Names of Amma — Sri Mata Amritanandamayi Ashtottara Shata Nama Stotram, composed by a great devotee, the late Sri Unni Nambootiripad. The stotram is based on Amma's divine life. To start with, I was in a dilemma as to how I could find time for writing the play, since there was no one to help me in the day-to-day activities of the ashram. But to my great surprise, a thirty-five-year old woman approached me and expressed her desire to stay with me in the ashram for a while. I was overjoyed to think that Amma had brought her when I needed help the most. She was very good at taking down dictations. When the writing was completed she took leave of me. The divine drama of Amma's life, as depicted in the stotram, was divided into various sections — Amma's Absolute nature (*Poornabrahma Swarupam*), birth and

Oṁ Śiva-Śaktyaikya Rūpiṇyai Namaḥ

---

childhood, Sri Krishna Sadhana, Devi Sadhana, Sri Krishna Bhava darshan, Devi Bhava darshan, Amma as the Supreme Teacher, establishing the Math, various humanitarian activities, etc. It required sixty characters to enact the scenes. I gave music to the stotram with the help of the music teacher of the school, and recorded the play with the facilities available in the ashram. When it was time for rehearsal, I again felt the need for helping hands. Then I remembered Sreedevi (an Australian devotee), who had been in Amritapuri for a few months and who had volunteered to come and help me in case I needed her. Since Amma was on a foreign tour at that time it was impossible for me to seek Her direct permission for calling Sreedevi. One day, I was praying to Amma for guidance in front of one of Her photographs, when the phone rang and I found that it was Sreedevi who had called me. Amma, who is omniscient and omnipresent, had heard my prayers and had answered me. I told Sreedevi to come immediately. I felt that even equipment like telephones are mediations of Her divine plans. I found Sreedevi very helpful, especially during the rehearsal of the drama. I was fortunate to receive similar experiences throughout. With the help of teachers and students of Amrita Vidyalayam and other benefactors I presented the play which extended for an hour, as a pada puja to Amma on the first day of the festival.

After the festival was over, while we were engaged in rearranging the ashram, I happened to see heaps of ropes in the courtyard even after the pantal had been dismantled. Perhaps they had been carelessly left behind by the workers. I then recollected Amma's advice given to me in Amritapuri. Amma had told me, "My child, if you see ropes lying abandoned here and there, collect them and keep them in the store room." Then She had added, "In my childhood days I used to attend the Oachira temple festival with my parents. At that time in order to make a monetary offering in the temple I used to make ropes from the green coconut husks with my own hands and sell them." Those ropes which Amma's tender hands had made in Her childhood continue to give the creative force to Her ashrams, temples and many other institutions in the present time. Amma's exhortation is that festivities must be disciplined enjoyment, organised with frugality,

Oṁ Śiva-Śaktyaikya Rūpiṇyai Namaḥ

and service-mindedness, communication of eternal values etc., should be their hallmarks. May Amma elevate human minds through the festivals which emanate higher values in society.

Oṁ Namaḥ Śivāya

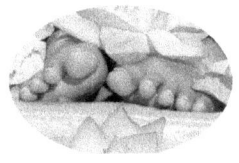

Oṁ Amṛteśwaryai Namaḥ

Chapter 4

Amma – The Sum Total of Divine Energy

During one of Her early Delhi visits Amma took up a one-day pilgrimage to Haridwar and Rishikesh, thus fulfilling a long cherished desire of the ashramites and devotees. Early in the morning She proceeded to Haridwar with the ashramites. She gave me the privilege of serving Her during the trip. Amma and Her children prepared themselves to take a dip in the crystal clear, glossy, azure waters of the holy river Ganga in Haridwar. Amma cautioned us to hold onto the protective steel bars installed in the river to safeguard ourselves from the strong water currents. Soon all of us finished our holy dip and came out of the river, but Amma was still standing in the freezing cold water of the Ganga in samadhi (transcendent absorption in the Supreme). Amma was completely oblivious of the outside world and was standing still in the cold water for several hours. Finally, a few of the ashramites gently lifted Her up, carried Her in their arms and laid Her down on a mat on the ground. I sat beside Her and massaged Her holy feet and body, chanting the 'Om Namah Śivaya' mantra. I was in tears when I recollected Amma's earlier words prior to the North Indian tour regarding Her bathing in the holy river. While conversing with Amma in Her room in Amritapuri, I had expressed my wish that She should take a dip in the holy Ganga and revive the sanctity of the river. Then She had replied, "Once Amma goes into the Ganga, She may not come back." The memory of that prediction and the long samadhi with no breathing and very feeble heart beats made me pray continuously with an aching heart: "Amma, shower mercy on your children and come back to us." Group chanting of 'Om Namah Śivaya' mantra continued for a long while. At last, out of compassion for Her children,

Amma — The Sum Total of Divine Energy

Amma woke up to the outside world, and after a while expressed Her displeasure at being pulled away from Mother Ganga. Thereafter, somehow, Amma got ready to travel to Rishikesh in Her car, followed by the ashramites and devotees. It was evening when we reached Rishikesh, travelling along the steep mountain roads. Here all of us meditated with Amma on the rocks by the Ganga and sang evening bhajans. Later, She visited some of the local ashrams at the request of the ashramites there, and blessed them. Soon after, She returned to Delhi with Her children.

I had many golden opportunities of witnessing Her ecstatic dancing and samadhi, during the early days of my ashram life. At that time, on the non- Bhava darshan days, after the evening bhajans, Amma used to sit alone or lie down in the ashram courtyard. None of the ashramites would disturb Her solitude then. One night, after bhajans and a light dinner, I went to Amma's room upstairs. From the southern balcony I looked out and saw Her dancing by the side of the pond near the backwaters. The pond and its surroundings, dotted with coconut trees, were bathed in moonlight. Amma's exquisitely graceful steps were echoing softly in the moonlit courtyard and surrounding areas. It was as if the full moon of divine love was rising high in the ocean of *chitananda* (absolute knowledge and bliss). Immediately, I climbed down the stairs and went near Her. Amma then came dancing to the front yard of the Kalari (the small, old darshan temple) and the Vedanta Vidyalaya room. Using Her sari as a dhoti and singing many bhajans, like "Radharamana mama hridayesha", Amma danced for a long time and then laid Herself down on the ground. She was in samadhi. I sat near Her and placed Her head on my lap, enjoying a rare bliss as I chanted my mantra mentally. After a long time, Amma got up and walked towards Her room. I followed Her. On the veranda in front of Her room She lay down with Her Holy feet on my lap. She was devoid of outward consciousness. I sat meditating on Amma's divine form and had a rare vision of many cosmic spheres rising and setting in the reddish effulgence emitted from Her body. That transcendental vision given by Amma – the embodiment of scriptural truths - awakened in me the import of the twelfth mantra of Sri Lalita Sahasranamavali – 'Oṁ nijāruṇa prabhā pūra majjad brahmāṇḍa maṇḍalāyai namaḥ' (Salutations to the Divine Mother who immerses the entire universe in the red effulgence of Her form). I was convinced that Amma is the power that keeps the entire universe intent on action. It was late at night when Amma got up and went to Her room. The rest of the night I spent in Her divine presence, in Her service.

Till the year 1995 Amma took me along with Her during the Indian tours and gave me many spiritual lessons which made my ashram life fruitful. Once while travelling in Kerala, a bhajan cassette was being played in the bus. One of the bhajans was based on the intense divine love of Sri Krishna – the God incarnate–for Sri Radha–His eternal beloved and devotee. While listening to it I remembered a verse from the eleventh ashtapadi (*Gita Govindam*) in which Radha's companion is reminding her of Sri Krishna's deep love for her. She says, "O Radha, Krishna is waiting impatiently for you in Vrindavan. When the birds flutter their wings and the leaves sway in the breeze, He imagines that you are on your way to meet Him and looks intently towards the path you take." While pondering on it, a doubt cropped up in my mind: "Does Amma, who is the embodiment of Sri Krishna, manifest such an intense love in Her present incarnation?" – and I expressed my thought to Her. She answered the question later during the next Indian tour. One afternoon, Amma and the ashramites were sitting on the shore of the river Tunga Bhadra in Karnataka after taking a bath in the river. One of the ashram vehicles was yet to reach there, and Amma with Her children sat meditating while waiting for it to arrive. I was sitting next to Amma serving Her. Along the highway, vehicles were coming and going, and She looked towards the road with unusual anxiety at the sound of each vehicle. I realised that Amma, who is omniscient, knew very well what might have happened to the vehicle and Her over-anxiety was nothing but an expression of Her deep concern for Her children. It was also meant to clear my doubt about Her love. By Her grace, the bus that had been delayed arrived soon without any serious mishaps, and we continued the journey. When we reached a suitable spot, Amma asked us to stop for dinner. All of us received the food plates from Her and were taking the prasad when She spoke, looking at me. "Now (in Amma's present incarnation) Amma is anxiously awaiting Her children every moment." This unexpected explanation given by Her removed all my doubts. On a later occasion, Amma, the power behind body, mind and intellect, gave me another experience to show how She showers Her divine love continuously on Her children. One night I experienced intolerable pain in the urethra without any obvious reasons. Any movement of the body, even respiration, increased the pain. When I cried and prayed to Amma, the pain subsided miraculously after a while. This experience also revealed to me that Amma is the sole refuge for all the beings enslaved by the body, which is the seat of not only pain and pleasure but also birth and death.

Once while travelling from Karnataka to Pune, no lunch was kept ready in the vehicle to be served on the way. When we reached Goa, Amma instructed us to have lunch from a hotel, and all the ashramites obeyed Her while Amma and I remained in the car. She had a light lunch in the car and I was about to have my meal brought by a brahmachari[7] for me from the hotel, when She told me to save the curd (yogurt) for Her. After a while the brahmachari came and told me that I could have the curd and he would bring another cup for Amma. But I did not pay any attention to his words and finished my meal without curd as Amma had instructed. When he came again I enquired about Amma's curd and found out that he could not procure it because the stock had finished in the hotel. I did not feel bad in the least and prostrated at Her Holy feet mentally for saving me from the peril of disobedience. After lunch we continued the journey to Pune, and on the way, late at night, Amma and a few brahmacharinis including me had to halt in a totally unfamiliar house. In those days the ashram had no branches in North India and hence, during the tour, Amma and the ashramites stayed in houses and various public places. As soon as She reached the house, as usual She climbed up the stairs to the roof to rest there and I followed Her. Amma appeared to be in Guru bhava (the mood of the spiritual teacher) and completely indrawn. She lay

---

[7] Later he left the ashram.

down on a mat spread on the floor and I sat at Her Lotus Feet. After some time, Amma wanted to take some food. While I was serving Her She specifically reminded me of the curd which, by Her grace, I could procure immediately. I realised that Amma was giving me a surprise test by insisting on saving the curd, and by Her grace I could get through it successfully. After food She rested there. I sat beside Her, silently meditating on the many divine 'lilas' which Amma - who is 'Lila Vinodini'[8] (She who delights in divine sport) - had played with me.

By Amma's grace, I had many golden opportunities during the tours when She further revealed Her supreme divine nature to me. In Kollur Mookambika temple, installed by Sri Sankara Bhagavadpada, Amma revealed Her identity with the deity there. One evening, along with the ashramites, She took a dip in the holy river Sowparnika and meditated sitting on the rocks by the river. She returned to the residence after giving permission to the ashramites to have darshan in the temple. I followed Amma and remained with

---

[8] Lalita Sahasranāmam, 966

Her for the night. It was a day of rest for Amma during the busy tour. While She lay down completely absorbed in Her Self, I engaged myself in service of Her holy feet. By Amma's grace, a clear picture of the Divine Mother Mookambika came to my mind. I mentally prayed to Her, "Amma, if you are one with Sri Mookambika, kindly show Yourself in Her form with your right foot kept on your left knee." Immediately Amma responded to my prayer, getting into the form that I wished to see! I was transported to a higher mental state and remained immersed in Amma for a long time.

When Amma visited Rameswaram for the first time, about fifty disciples went with Her. Food and accommodation were provided in the Sri Ramakrishna Tapovan ashram. In the morning, Amma and Her children meditated on the shores of the tranquil ocean, followed by a visit to the Shiva temple. Standing in front of the sanctum-sanctorum, Amma said, "I have brought our children to you" - which sounded to me like a divine dialogue between the universal parents! Later, Amma sanctified the twenty-two holy wells in the temple yard by Her divine presence.

Amma — The Sum Total of Divine Energy

Once, during the annual festival of the Chennai Brahmasthanam temple, Amma was giving darshan on the temporarily constructed stage in the pantal. When the darshan was about to finish I stood waiting for Amma on the veranda of Her room, on the first floor of the ashram building. While I was looking at Her divine form and chanting my mantra, a childish thought cropped up in my mind: "Amma is verily the Goddess *Kāli*. Why then does She not have reddish eyebrows as seen in the idol?" Soon the darshan was over and Amma got up and walked along the path on the left side of the pantal towards Her room, accompanied by a few of Her children. Prostrating to Amma mentally, I kept my gaze fixed on Her. I noticed that, as usual, the top of Amma's garment was soiled with the sweat and tears of the people who had come for darshan. But what was unusual on that day was that the vermillion from Her tilak had spread to Her eyebrows, making them reddish in colour! I felt that the revelation which Amma gave as a response to the random thought of mine was an illustration of Her divine motherly love for Her innocent children like me.

One morning, during the return journey from Kolkata after various spiritual programmes there, Amma gave Her consent to the ashramites to visit the famous *Bhavatāriṇi* temple in Dakshineshwar, and Belur Math. I stayed back with Amma (who remained alone in the bus) since I had been to those holy places earlier. After a while, She alighted from the bus and started to walk forward. I followed Her. Pappettan (Sri Padmanabhan) wanted to show Amma the way to the temple, but She proceeded on Her own, reached the Panchavati in the temple yard and remained there under the amala tree for a while. It was as if Amma were revelling in Her own world. After strolling in the Panchavati and along the shore of the river Ganga, She proceeded by Herself to the temple of Bhavatarini, the Divine Mother. It was the time of 'arati' (the worship with lighted lamps and camphor to conclude the routine morning and evening poojas). Amma - who is Avatarini and Bhavatarini - stood in front of the shrine sanctifying the pooja and blessing the temple priests. After some time, She came back and sat in the bus, and when the ashram children returned, resumed the journey. The unique pilgrimage that I had with Amma had filled my mind with an ineffable joy and peace. While sitting in the bus in Her holy presence a divine drama was being enacted in my mind. Various scenes flashed through my mind, one after another. The mental picture became very bright, of Mother Kali dancing in bliss with swaying steps on the roof of the Bhavatarini temple, and Sri Ramakrishna calling out to Her in Bhavasamadhi, "O Mother, please don't come towards the edge, you may fall down!". The form of Sri Sarada Devi, as I had seen in the shrine of Her temple in Jayrambati, Her birth place, came to my mind vividly. Then the all-inclusive form of Amma giving darshan to Her children in Her darshan hut in Amritapuri appeared in my mind. That clear vision of Amma as *Pūrṇa brahma svarūpiṇi*' (the complete manifestation of Absolute Truth) enabled me to get immersed in meditation for a long time, until I was called to receive lunch from Amma's holy hands. While giving prasad, Amma advised me, "Try to remain in a similar state of mind always and everywhere." I prostrated again and again at the feet of Amma, *Sarvadevadevī svarūpiṇi* (the Universal Mother who is the embodiment of all Gods and Goddesses) and eagerly partook of the prasad.

Oṁ Namaḥ Śivāya

Oṁ Amṛteśwaryai Namaḥ

Chapter 5

Oṁ Nāma Pārāyaṇa Prītāyai Namaḥ[9]

Right from the inception of the ashram, while ministering to the spiritual needs of the ashramites, Amma exhorted them to imbibe the importance of japa sadhana (repetition of holy mantras and names). Even before I had joined the ashram, in Her first letter written to me while I was engaged in medical service in the Sri Ramakrishna Ashram Hospital at Thiruvananthapuram, She had written, "My darling daughter, Amma knows that

---

[9] Sri Lalita Sahasranamavali, mantra 732: Salutations to the Divine Mother who is pleased by the repetition of Her names (any name of God).

there is no one to assist you there and at times you become stressed and dejected. If you chant your mantra, you will be mentally and spiritually rejuvenated." Those nectarine words were consoling and inspiring to me. Very soon, with Amma's blessings I was in Amritapuri, and was enchanted by Amma's darshan and Her repetition of "Shiva, Shiva". Later when I became a member of the ashram, I heard directly from Amma about Her Sri Krishna sadhana. She told me, "My child, when Amma wished to have a direct vision of Sri Krishna, day and night I chanted 'Krishna, Krishna'. While engaged in household chores I did not let any moment pass by without Nama japa. While walking, 'one Name with one step' was the rule. If I happened to forget, I took two steps backwards to correct the mistake and continued the japa. When I cooked rice, I kept a target number of mantras to be chanted by the time the rice was cooked." This sadhana leela of Amma was to set an example for Her children to inculcate in them the importance of love for God's Name.

One day during my early days in the ashram, I was with Amma in Her room. She told me, "I shall initiate you today with a holy mantra." On hearing Her words, a doubt arose in my mind — do I need to be initiated again since I already have a mantra? She reassured me by saying, "Amma will give you the same mantra." In the evening when the bhavadarsan started, I sat meditating in the Kalari in Amma's divine presence. When the bhavadarshan got over, Amma made me sit on Her own seat in the Kalari, which was saturated with divine vibrations, and initiated me, making it clear that the mantra is not to be repeated mechanically. It has to be a constant thought in the mind and part of day-to-day life. *'Mananāt trāyate iti mantraḥ'* ('the sacred words will protect one when continuously contemplated upon'). By encouraging the constant chanting of the mantra mentally, Amma saves Her children from many conflicts and crises arising in daily life. Usually a mantra is seen to have three parts — 'OM' (the all pervading consciousness), the Name of the Beloved Deity and 'Namah' (the word of surrender which enables the individual to identify with the Absolute). A drop of water gains the depth and vastness of the ocean when it becomes one with it. Likewise, one can gain infinite strength, peace and bliss by surrendering to the Almighty. Amma always advised me to make the extroverted mind introverted with the help of the mantra. With a one-pointed mind a student can study well, a scientist can become more focused on his scientific research, an artist can excel in his artistic creation and a musician can bring out the best in himself. "O my children, God is not somewhere high up in the sky, but everywhere and in every being, endowing the body with life and activity. Amma does not expect anyone to worship Her. She only wants you to know your own real nature. God is really without any name or form. The names and forms are only for your easy perception. One can worship God in any name and form according to one's liking. But it has to be kept in mind that one has to stick to one name and form at all times." Amma made me aware of the great potency of chanting the mantra while I was doing public service in the Ashram Centre in the Triprayar area of Thrissur district. One evening, as usual, I was sitting in the ashram courtyard under a coconut tree chanting my mantra mentally. At that time Dr. Nalini, a close devotee of Amma, called me on the phone.

She told me that her cousin had passed away and she was leaving for his house in Kannur, so she could not come to visit me as planned previously. On hearing the news, I started praying for the departed cousin of Dr. Nalini and continued the mantra japa. Soon my attention was diverted to two young ashramites sitting on the veranda of the ashram building and talking. I thought I would go to them and request them to do japa for the departed soul. I did so and came back to find that a huge, heavy frond from the coconut tree had fallen down exactly on the spot where I had been sitting. If I had not gotten up from there in time, that unusually large frond would have fallen on my head and even endangered my life. I understood that Amma had saved me only because I had been doing japa for that departed brother and prompted others also to do so. Amma also made me aware of the fact that death is at the door of each and everyone at all times, and when we help others we are helping ourselves. Again I focused my mind on Amma, the indwelling Self, and continued doing mantra japa, which is an all-powerful remedy.

Oṁ Nāma Pārāyaṇa Prītāyai Namaḥ

Amma gave me two valuable experiences which revealed the greatness of the 'Om Namah Śivaya' mantra, while I was working in the Triprayar area. It was this mantra that rescued Shanta from the jaws of death. Her son was well-employed in one of the Gulf countries. His parents were making preparations for his wedding ceremony. Unfortunately, the boy met with an accident and passed away. When Shanta came to know about the tragedy she was so grief stricken that she was unable to move out of her room. She could neither eat nor drink nor look after her daily needs. She could not speak to anybody. As days passed by, her condition steadily deteriorated. It was in the course of 'Amrita Sauhrita Yajnam', which involved spreading Amma's message of love and service in each and every house, that we were guided to Shanta's house. The whole house was seen enveloped in gloom. Shanta's mother was on her deathbed with geriatric problems. Only the young children in that joint family were displaying some signs of life, and their interaction with us was encouraging. We lighted the sacred lamp in the house, chanting the mantra. A simple pooja was performed and bhajans commenced with the song 'Bandhamilla bhandhuvilla swantam-allonnum' ('at the last moment, only the atman, the indwelling Self, remains as your own'). Then we chanted 'Om Namah Śivaya' for a while, in which the children participated enthusiastically. They clearly appeared to be enjoying it. When it was time for us to leave I told the children, "O my friends, continue chanting 'Om Namah Śivaya', which will make you and others at home, happy and peaceful. They did accordingly, thereby transforming the whole atmosphere from hell to heaven. Later on I came to know that with Amma's blessing all had turned out well after our short visit, the pooja, prayers and 'Namah Śivaya' chanting. Shanta, who had stopped caring for food, drink and her daily routine, had come back to her normal self. When Amma returned from the west, Shanta came to Amritapuri and had Her darshan. Amma blessed her by initiating her into mantra japa. The power of Amma's love and the mantra made the river of Shanta's life flow again and helped it to regain its pristine beauty. Shanta's mother also was liberated from her miserable life by the power of 'Namah Śivaya' mantra. One evening Shanta's brother came to the ashram and

Oṁ Nāma Pārāyaṇa Prītāyai Namaḥ

told me about their mother. She was neither alive nor dead and was in great misery. I instructed him to pray to Amma and chant 'Om Namah Śivaya' continuously along with other members of the family. They did 'Namah Śivaya' japa, which, along with the prayers from their hearts ended the suffering of Shanta's mother. She had a peaceful death the following evening.

The 'Namah Śivaya' revolution of Amma spread around the whole world, breaking all barriers. Not only devotees of Amma, but all those who come into contact with Her from various institutions accept 'Namah Śivaya' mantra as part and parcel of their life. The mantra said with different intonations now replaces mundane usages like 'hello, o.k., Hi' etc,. It is also used to call out to someone at a distance, politely ask a person to keep quiet, etc. Amma gives an opportunity even to the so-called modern people to hear and comprehend the uniqueness of Namah Śivaya. One night, Amma visited a house, while She was in Delhi conducting various spiritual programmes. The family members had heard about Her from their relatives, and invited Her to their house with the hope that She would help them to solve their problems. That wealthy family had a western lifestyle. Though ignorant of the Indian way of worshipping a spiritual teacher, they received Amma and Her disciples in the traditional way with the help of Her devotees. They had arranged a special chair for Her to be seated in, while they performed the pada-puja (worship of Her holy feet) to the accompaniment of Vedic mantras recited by the ashramites. That night, along with a few of Her children, Amma stayed in the house and blessed the family. The next day, after my morning routine, I went to the drawing room to sit there and chant the Sri Lalita Sahasranamam. But a surprising sight awaited me there. I saw one of the dogs of the house sitting on Amma's pada-pooja chair! I felt very bad and brought the matter to the notice of the lady of the house. She told me, "the dog is diabetic. So we leave her alone." "Why not keep a separate chair for your dog?" I asked her. "She is allowed to sit on any of the chairs," she said indifferently and went away. Then I prostrated to Amma's chair and looking at the dog said, "Om Namah Śivaya". To my utter surprise the dog immediately jumped down from the chair and sat in a posture of prostration! Then I told one girl who was with me there to repeat 'Namah Śivaya', and the dog responded in the same manner. All those who were present there watched the scene in awe and wonder. Then the daughter of the house also came there, and on my request tried to say 'Namah Śivaya' to the dog. It was difficult for her to even pronounce the mantra properly, yet she managed to speak it out in an English accent. Her darling dog responded as before by stretching its fore-paws in namaskar. The daughter started to believe the potency of 'Namah Śivaya,' may be due to her love for her darling dog. I felt that Amma influences even pet animals like dogs with the mantra. Later on the whole family grew close to Amma and a change came in their lifestyle. Soon thereafter, the girl came to Amritapuri with her parents and received a mantra from Amma.

Amma encourages Her children to engage themselves in constant remembrance of God's Name instead of wasting their time in idle talk, and to be free from worries and tensions of daily life. To please Amma, who is '*Nāma pārāyaṇaprītā*,' the best methods available are Nama japa and selfless service. One morning during the early years of my ashram life, I was sitting in the meditation room and doing 'Sahasranamarchana' (chanting of the Thousand Names of the Divine Mother while mentally offering flowers with each mantra). That day for some reason only a few of the ashramites were there for the archana. Soon after the archana had started, Amma came down from Her room, which was just above the meditation room. Amma was very pleased, and after the archana She called me and said, "Leelamol, you have to lead the archana every morning". I did accordingly for a few years that followed. Amma encouraged ashramites, including western residents, to receive visitors with a smile, mentally saying, 'Namah Śivaya', seeing God in them, and to not be alarmed by huge crowds, especially during darshan days.

Scriptures also proclaim the importance of singing God's Name:

> *Nāham Vasāmi Vaikuṇṭhe*
> *Naca Yogi hṛdaye*
> *Yatra madbhaktāḥ gāyanti*
> *Tatra Tiṣṭhāmi Nārada*

Vishnu Puranam

O Narada, I do not reside in Vaikuntha or in the hearts of the yogis. I will be especially present there where my devotees sing my praises — so says Bhagavan in the Vishnu Puranam.

The great sage Narada, an unparalleled devotee of Sri Maha Vishnu, continuously plays on his Veena while chanting the name 'Narayana, Narayana', and travels around the whole world purifying the cosmic atmosphere. Amma observes that Narada always aimed at the betterment of the whole world, though he is blamed as an instigator by those ignorant of his greatness. Sri Narada considers the Gopikas (illiterate cowherd women of Vrindavan) as the paragons of supreme devotion (Narada Bhakti Sutras, 1:21). Amma says that the Gopikas lived a life of ordinary milkmaids and yet attained a higher state than the great sages by their total surrender to Sri Krishna. While looking after their households they could unswervingly fix their minds on their beloved. Amma also points out that their devotion was so great that they wrote names like 'Krishna, Mukunda, Murari' on their pots in the kitchen. While they walked along the streets to vend the milk and milk products, they called out, "Govinda, Damodara, Madhava" instead of milk, curd, butter, etc. This one-pointed concentration enabled them to reach the highest state. The story of Ajamila[10] in Srimad Bhagavatam also teaches us how great is the 'Narayana Nama'. Ajamila was a brahmin by birth. He lived the life of a traditional brahmin, leading a God-oriented life, until one day he happened to go to the forest to collect articles for a homa (fire ceremony). To his misfortune he got attracted to a prostitute who lived in the forest. He became so infatuated with this woman that he never returned home. He lived with her and had many children. Finally, the yamadootas (the messengers from the world of death) came to take him away. He was so scared that he started crying, and suddenly he called out to his last son 'Narayana' who was still a child, thinking that he may become scared of the yamadootas. His calling of God's Name, even though accidental, saved him from the jaws of death. The messengers of Maha Vishnu appeared on the scene and they defeated those from the world of death in a debate and saved Ajamila. Simultaneously, Ajamila's place in the forest was

---

[10] Srimad Bhagavatam 6: 1, 2, 3

miraculously transformed. That place, a veritable hell, turned into heaven on earth. Such is the power of the name 'Narayana'. Ajamila, on his deathbed, had consciously witnessed arguments between the messengers of the two forces —life and death- and he became a changed person. He decided to discontinue his forest life with the prostitute and started a new form of austere forest life. In due course he attained liberation from birth and death, sorrows and miseries, and reached the blissful abode of Maha Vishnu – Vaikuntha.

Sri Chaitanya teaches us that in the present age nothing other than Hari Nama (God's Name) leads one to liberation:

Harernāma harernāma harernāmaiva kevalam
Kalau nāstyeva nāstyeva nāstyeva gatiranyathā

He also prays on behalf of ordinary human beings, "O Bhagavan, you have innumerable Names and you have filled each of them with your immense divine power. They can be chanted at all possible times. Your compassion is infinite and so is my misfortune that I am born devoid of true love for your Names."

Many people ask Amma why Nama japa fails to give the desired results. Amma explains, "A medicine, though potent, will be effective only when taken as per the instructions of the physician. Some dietary restrictions may also have to be observed." Same is the case of Nama japa, which is an all-powerful remedy and as sweet as nectar. But it becomes futile when combined with negative activities – the *Nāmāparādhās*. It is like keeping sugar on one side and inviting the ants from the other side. The *Nāmāparādhās* are: disrespect to the Great Ones, spiritual teachers, scriptural texts like the Vedas, Puranas, etc.; committing sins and trying to cover them up with Nama japa; doubting the efficacy of Divine Names; comparing Nama japa to various rites and rituals; initiating the undeserving to Nama japa; lack of one-pointed attention in japa; indulgence in sensual pleasures; pride and egoism; inability to see the various Divine Names as one. O Amma, kindly keep me away from all negativities and grant me true love for you and your Divine Names. May I bow down again and again at your lotus feet.

Oṁ Namaḥ Śivāya

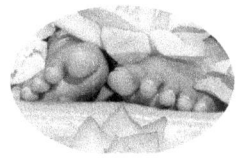

Oṁ Amṛteśwaryai Namaḥ

Chapter 6

Mṛtyor mā Amṛtaṁ Gamaya[11]

Amma eradicates not only the mental and physical diseases of Her children but also "bhavaroga" — the disease of the cycle of birth and death. She inspires Her children to realise the true Self which lasts even after the body perishes. The Upanishads also speak about the immortal nature of the atman — the indwelling Self. Sri Sankara points out that human life is transitory like a drop of dew on a lotus petal and the aim of life is to seek God. Amma shows Her children the way to immortality. She is the Divine Mother

---

[11] Lead me from death to immortality.

who removes all diseases and sorrows of Her children and bestows on them health, longevity and liberation. During the early days of the ashram, Amma cured diseases mostly by Her divine will (Sankalpa). Before going to the ashram while I was in medical service in Thiruvananthapuram, I suffered from urticaria for a while and was treated with antihistamine tablets. Soon after I came to Amritapuri the skin disease started to trouble me again. I was scared to restart the antihistamine tablets since it would make me sleepy and hinder my daily spiritual practices. I took refuge in Amma and She consoled me saying, "My child, you don't have to take that medicine hereafter." Then She added, "Amma has kept the disease in control and not cured it completely since that is a connecting link between Amma and Her daughter." In the years that followed, by Her grace, I could avoid the medicine completely. In due course, I was convinced that the duty of a true disciple is to become an offering in the sacrificial fire of the Guru's humanitarian activities.

Occasionally, Amma used herbs like basil, turmeric, and pure rainwater, rosewater etc., to cure many of the ailments of Her children. Once during Bhava darshan, Amma gave me a valuable experience. On a particularly scorching day, a devotee came to Amma during Bhava darshan and prayed for a cure for her eye ailment which was found to be incurable by medicines. Amma asked her to bring some pure rainwater. Since it was very hot and had not rained for many days, a doubt came to my mind – "How is it possible to get rainwater in this weather?" I got a glimpse of the depth of Her divine will when I witnessed an unusually heavy rain during the following days. On the next Bhava darshan day, Amma blessed the rainwater brought by the devotee and she was soon cured. One night during the early period of my ashram life I noticed that I had a large painful boil posterior on my buttock. A thought came to my mind that I was helpless since there was no one to give me medical assistance. But to my great surprise, a nurse came to me unexpectedly, introduced herself, and told me that she had come for Bhava darshan that day. I realised that it was Amma who had brought her to me. She did the necessary dressing and left the following day. Not knowing who would continue to dress the boil subsequently, I prayed to Amma fervently in the night. When I woke up next morning, there was no trace of the boil! Once more, I was convinced that Amma never forsakes Her children who take refuge in Her.

I had the golden opportunity to witness personally how Amma showered Her divine grace on one of Her greatest devotees – Sri Ottur Unni Namboodiripad. Sri Ottur became an ashramite in 1983 at the age of 79 and began to worship Amma as God incarnate. He was a lifelong celibate, and a devotee of Sri Krishna since childhood. Later he was devoted to Sri Ramakrishna and engaged himself in rigorous sadhanas. He was a great Sanskrit scholar and a famous poet who devoted his life entirely to spiritual practices, scriptural studies and teaching. He was an authority on Srimad Bhagavatam and often conducted discourses in the famous Guruvayoor temple (Thrissur district) and in Amritapuri as well. Amma gave him Her own room to stay in and shifted to a small room near the Kalari. She used to call him 'Unnikannanmon' (darling child Krishna) and often took him along with Her to meditate on the seashore. After a few years of blissful life in Amritapuri in Amma's care, once Sri

Ottur suffered from an attack of severe diarrhoea. As per Amma's instructions, I administered I.V drips and necessary medicines to him. Sri Ottur appeared to be very upset thinking that the disease might become life-threatening and prayed to Amma – "Amma, kindly give me a few more years of life so that I can witness more of your divine life," and She granted his prayer. Thus he could continue his blessed life in Amritapuri for a few more years. He used to sit in deep meditation for a long time in the Kalari during Amma's Bhava darshan. Since he felt that it was improper for him to continue to stay in Her room, he shifted to a small room near the Kalari. Amma graciously allowed him to tour with Her in Kerala on many occasions. Once She visited his family and blessed his relatives. Soon after, Sri Ottur composed Mata Amritanandamayi Ashtottara Shata Namastotram – 108 names of Amma depicting Her divine life. This great hymn which illustrates the deep spiritual insight and extraordinary poetic talent of the author, may be divided into nine sections: Amma's Absolute nature – Poorna brahma swarupam (1-17), birth and childhood (18-33), Sri Krishna Sadhna and vision of Bhagavan (34-45),

Devi Sadhna and vision of the Divine Mother (46-55), Amma as the embodiment of all divine attributes (56-63), Sri Krishna Bhava darshan (64-68), Devi Bhava darshan (69-78), Amma as the Supreme teacher and founder of MA Math (79-93), various humanitarian activities (94-108). The daily chanting of these 108 names of Amma, describing Her divine life, continues to reverberate in the whole world. Sri Ottur felt that his life's end was nearing. He visited his family house and bid farewell to his family members and relatives and returned to the ashram before Amma's western tour. Weeping like a baby he prayed to Amma to keep him alive until She came back from the west. She assured him, "Until Amma comes back nothing will happen." Otturji, who was 85 years old, expressed his desire to undergo Ayurvedic treatment in Dr. Ramachandran Nair's house until Amma's return and She agreed.

Amma came back on August 17, 1989, from the west. Soon after, Sri Ottur also reached Amritapuri. In his last poem written on the day before his demise, Otturji expressed his desire to Amma, "The doctor has failed to cure me and the relatives have become desperate. O! Amma, kindly keep me on your lap and without delay take me from death to immortality." Late at night, after the Bhava darshan on 24th August, Amma visited him with a few of the ashramites, including me. She took Her darling son in Her holy hands and laid him on a new yellow silk mattress which had been recently offered to Her by a devotee. He implored Her, "Amma, kindly call me to you without delay." She remained with him for a while and entrusted me with the task of looking after him, before She left. The next morning, on the way to Otturji's room, I found a tender coconut in the kitchen. It was very unusual and I thought that Amma had kept it for Her darling son. I opened it, poured out the water into a cup and proceeded to Otturji's room. I found that his feet were slightly swollen with oedema and his breathing was somewhat laborious. I gave him the coconut water to drink in sips, thinking that it would help to eliminate oedema. Thereafter, he did not have anything else orally up to his last moment since he remained completely indrawn. It seemed that his only thought was that he was Amma's little child and he kept on telling us, "Bring Amma here." I replied, "You know how to bring Amma better than I." When he went on compelling me, I proceeded towards Amma's room to see whether the door was open. As soon as I was in front of the room, She Herself came and opened the door and let me in to be with Her for a while. I was amazed to see many of the physical ailments of Otturji reflected in Amma's body. It seemed that She was taking the suffering of Her "Otturmon" on Herself and allowing him to have a peaceful end. Amma allowed me to massage Her holy feet for a while and then told me, "Now you can go. I want to communicate with Unni." I understood that She was conversing with Her darling son in a subtle way and I took leave of Her. When I returned to Otturji's room, Amma's first disciple Br Amritatma Chaitanyaji (later Swami Amritaswarupananda Puri) was with him. One devotee, who used to listen to the Bhagavatam discourses of Sri Ottur in Guruvayoor regularly was also present there. Otturji was repeating his request, "Bring Amma." I felt that with those two words Sri Ottur was not only expressing his extreme inner yearning for Amma's vision but also his concern for the world at large. He was giving to one and all Amma's message "Don't delay to bring

Amma's true love and infinite compassion into your life." I noticed that his voice was becoming feeble and I was about to go to Amma's room again. But on the way, I was urgently called to see a patient. After attending to the patient I rushed to Otturji's room and found that Amma was already there. Her darling son, after having Her vision, had become one with Her – Poorna Brahma Swarupam – Her Supreme Reality. The body was soon taken to Amma's darshan hut where the chanting of Bhagavad Gita, Vishnu Sahasranamam and various other holy names went on during the whole day. Amma advised, "From the time of demise japa must go on with devotion avoiding unnecessary thoughts and speech. Only after three hours the jeeva (life force) fully detaches itself from the body. During this time a holy atmosphere has to be created with prayers and chanting." Sri Ottur had prayed to Amma that the cremation[12] should be done in Amritapuri. Hence the rites were duly performed by his nephew in Her divine presence, with ashramites and devotees taking part in them. Everyone felt that

---

[12] Antyeshti – the last of the 16 purification rites.

Amritapuri was submerged in the waves of the unique divine *leela* of Amma, who redeems Her children from the ocean of repeated births and deaths - *samsara* - and takes them to Her who is verily an ocean of *Amrita* - immortal bliss.

Actually, Amma had started Her first medical institution in Her divine abode, Amritapuri. It was a small free clinic for the ashramites and villagers which initially functioned in one of the small rooms under the ground floor of the *Kāli* temple. After a while, it was shifted to a spacious room in a one-storied building near the village path. While shifting, Amma came personally and blessed the clinic, participating in arranging medicines on the wooden racks. By Her divine grace, medicines used to come miraculously from many sources. A remarkable incident occurred in one house near the clinic, on the northern side of the ashram where Amma displayed Her first Krishna bhava. The man of that house was diagnosed with cancer of the lungs. He was treated in the cancer hospital, but he had to return home without being completely cured. He realised that Amma was his sole refuge, and She protected him from many complications of the disease and serious side effects of the cancer treatment. The medicines which were needed for symptomatic relief were made available for him from the clinic. With Amma's grace, cartons of medicines were 'discovered' in the clinic. I could not even trace from where they had come. The severe pain of the cancer was seen to subside with ordinary painkillers given from the clinic. It was as if Amma had accepted him as the first patient of the hospice in Badalapur, Mumbai, which was then in the making. Thus with Her blessings, he had a few more months of peaceful life in spite of the deadly disease. When Amma was leaving for Reunion and Mauritius islands, She stopped at his house and blessed him so that he may have a peaceful end. The next day at the same time, he left his body without suffering from the agony of death.

Once, Amma suddenly asked the Kollam devotees to organise a medical camp in the Kollam ashram, the first branch of MA Math. Two members of the Yuva Dharma Dhara (the youth wing of MA Math) ventured out to collect the required medicines. Initially they did not succeed. When the day of the camp was nearing, they came and told me, "We are not able to collect medicines though we are trying our best. We will have to buy some of the frequently used medicines." Since there was no other option, I gave them Rs 500 from the ashram office. I told them to be optimistic and try again, and that Amma would take care of everything. They did accordingly and surprisingly could collect medicines in abundance. On the morning of the camp, I left Amritapuri for Kollam in the ashram vehicle driven by a brahmachari who sceptically asked me, "Why do you want to go there? Not many patients are likely to come." "Let us carry out Amma's orders. She will be with us," I replied and we proceeded. I was confident that since Amma had given the medicines, She would bring the patients as well. We reached the venue with hope in our hearts. A few of the doctors who were Amma's devotees had also arrived to take part in the camp. With Her grace, there was a continuous flow of patients and the camp went on smoothly till evening. I continued to see patients even after other doctors left, and came back to Amritapuri late in the evening. In the hut, I had darshan of Amma, the Divine Mother who is verily the sole doer, apparently doing nothing. I offered myself at Her lotus feet and could remain in Her blissful presence for a while.

The devotee couple Shesha Iyer and Sampoornamma, known popularly in the ashram as 'Sheshacchan' and 'Pattiamma' were close devotees of Amma since 1984. They were earnestly looking for a Satguru (realised master) for a long time until they reached Amritapuri and accepted Amma as their spiritual master. Since they were the first devotees from Chennai, they were given the responsibility of organising various spiritual activities. Before coming to Amma they used to do sadhana in the temple of Mookambika in Kollur, Karnataka state, staying there for months together. Once early in the morning, while taking bath in the holy river Sowparnika, Sampoornamma lost her diamond ear ornaments in the river. It was dark and she found that it was impossible to recover them. She prayed to the Divine Mother, "If I find the lost ornaments, I will offer a diamond nose ring to you." With the Divine Mother's grace, she later recovered the earrings. Soon after that incident, they became Amma's devotees and started to visit Amritapuri regularly. They had forgotten all about the promised offering to Devi

Mookambika. During their third visit to Amritapuri, Amma suddenly asked Sampoornamma, "Where is the nose ring which you promised to give me?" They were stunned at Amma's question and sorry for their mistake. Thereafter, realising that Amma was Mookambika Devi Herself, they offered a newly made diamond nose ring to Her which She used to wear constantly. Pattiamma and Sheshacchan were very regular in their sadhana and became permanent residents of the ashram from 1990. They were very service minded and actively participated in various ashram activities. It was strange that while leading a blissful life in the ashram Pattiamma often expressed her desire to die. She might have thought that Amma would give her liberation after death or she might have been nearing death according to her horoscope. Whatever it might be, she became seriously ill at the age of 68. She was suffering from an intractable cough and on examination, I found that she had a heart problem also. She did not improve with the treatment in the private hospital in Karunagapally. She was indifferent to her physical ailments as well as to the treatment. Sheshacchan and other family members decided to take her to Chennai and to admit her to Apollo Hospital there. At that time, Amma was on the Indian tour and I was unable to contact Her. Without delay we got her discharged from the hospital and drove her to Thiruvananthapuram airport with an IV Line on her arm. Sheshacchan, myself and one brahmacharini who had previously been a nurse were in the car with Pattiamma. By Amma's grace, we reached the airport safely. At the airport, Pattiamma wanted to use the toilet and I requested her to go to one close-by. She did not take me seriously and went to one a little far away with the other brahmacharini. I was worried and kept the emergency life-saving medicines ready with me. She took an unduly long time in the toilet, using the wash basin etc. As soon as she came back, she fell unconscious. Immediately I injected the medicines and with Amma's grace, she came back to life. Everyone felt that it would be dangerous to take her all the way to Chennai. so we had to admit her to the Medical College Hospital, TVM, nearby. All of us including Pattiamma had a very tough time in the general ward of the teaching hospital. Meanwhile, to make matters worse, the patient developed acute non-functioning of the stomach and intestine. To our great misfortune the head of the unit was found to be most indifferent and inefficient. While we were going through such disheartening difficulties, Pattiamma disclosed to me for the first time that she had a lump in the groin. On examination, I found that she had an 'obstructed hernia' which was the cause of the acute shutdown of the abdomen. Immediately I conveyed the matter to the chief of the unit but alas! His response was indifferent. The condition of the patient was becoming worse day by day. I remembered that Pattiamma used to pray to Amma for death. I was convinced that Amma who is 'Sarva Mrityu Nivarini'[13] – the Divine Mother who guards Her devotees against death – only could save her. I decided to go to the ashram and pray to Amma who had returned from the Indian tour. In the ashram, I had Amma's dharshan and offered my prayers. Very soon, with Her blessings, we shifted Pattiamma to the Cosmopolitan Hospital with the help of the devotees in TVM, and without any further delay emergency abdominal surgery

---

[13] Sri Lalita Sahasranama, stotram 552

was performed. She recovered completely within a few days and returned to the ashram. I realised that one has to be very careful while praying to Amma, from Pattiamma's experience and from that of another devotee in Karunagapally. I had heard her telling Amma during Bhava darshan that she was fed up with life and wished to die. It so happened that soon after, she suffered from an attack of acute diarrhoea and had to undergo treatment in a hospital. She was cured but soon was laid up with life-threatening allergic reaction to the drugs. She recovered only after she mentally accepted her mistake and prayed to Amma for forgiveness.

It was before the starting of Amrita Kripa Hospital in Amritapuri that an old woman, Sumatiamma became a resident of the ashram. She had no family or relatives to help her. She was close to a devotee who brought her to the ashram, and on his request, Amma accepted her and gave her a room to stay in. After a few days, she had severe loose motion, the cause of which might have been ingestion of old Triphala powder infested with fungus. I came to know about it only when Amma called me on a Bhava darshan night and asked me to take her to the hospital immediately. I rushed to her room and found her in a state of collapse. With Amma's grace, I got a conveyance immediately and with a brahmacharini to accompany me, soon reached the hospital with Sumatiamma. We took care of the patient during the night. She became conscious and the diarrhoea came under control. As soon as she regained strength, she started scolding us for no valid reason. Somehow we managed to return to the ashram before Amma left for the West and luckily we had Her Dharshan. After a few days, Sumatiamma became seriously sick again. One of her legs which had been swollen with elephantiasis got infected and pus started pouring out. Symptoms of anaemia and urinary infection worsened the situation. Very soon I had to take her to the Sri Ramakrishna Ashram Hospital, TVM, with which I was familiar. There the necessary treatment and the incessant scolding of the patient went on simultaneously. Since the patient was not ambulant, she needed help even for her daily routine activities. Initially, help came from Amritapuri and the patient was becoming better. Yet she was reluctant to get up from the bed. No one was willing to be with her because of her stubborn nature and continuous scolding. Finally, when I was alone with her, I prayed to Amma and by Her grace, the TVM devotees extended their help. When her physical condition was becoming better, I took the patient back to Amritapuri. When Amma returned from the West, I had Her darshan and I offered myself and the patient at Her Lotus Feet. By Her grace, after a few months of nursing in the Amritapuri clinic, the patient regained her normal health. All the while she had been non-cooperative and quarrelsome. A change for the better came in her when she knew that Amma was going to initiate me into sannyasa (monastic life) that year (1994). She came to me and prostrated at my feet, repenting her earlier behaviour. I realised that the whole ordeal that Amma had given me was to prepare me for monastic life. By Her grace, I could cross the morass of abuses and become one of the monastic disciples of Amma, who is the infinite ocean of compassion. Amma, I pray to you to kindly make my flight towards Your Lotus Feet easy and fast.

Oṁ Namaḥ Śivāya

Oṁ Amṛteśvaryai Namaḥ

Chapter 7

Amma – The Inner Guide

Amma graciously gave me the first opportunity to participate in Her birthday celebrations in the year 1985. On the previous night, Amma and the ashram children went to the seashore to fetch sand to be spread in the ashram front yard. It was a unique experience to be on the seashore with Amma, in whose divine effulgence the hearts of Her children open up. While filling the bags with sand, Amma said, "The Gurus in the past also used to engage themselves in similar activities." While walking to the ashram with sand bags I remembered the experience I had on Amma's

previous birthday while I was in Thiruvananthapuram. Though I had an intense yearning to participate in the celebrations I was unable to do so. I prayed to Amma, "I am so sad that I can't take leave from my work and come to you now. You are omniscient and must be aware of it. Kindly enlighten me about the various programmes of the day through someone." The very next morning that prayer was answered miraculously. To my surprise, I heard one devotee of Amma talking in detail about various programmes including the release of the ashram's monthly magazine. My heart was filled with an ineffable joy which Amma had imparted by fulfilling the small wish of this little child of Hers. I became fully convinced that this was Amma's way of answering my prayers, which in turn awakened in me the indelible feeling of the Divine Mother's omniscience, love and compassion.

The sand was spread in the yard making it ready to welcome the devotees. Amma's birthday celebrations started early in the morning on Thursday, the 3rd of October with group singing of divine names and bhajans in the streets of the village. The programme in the ashram began with the Guru pada puja (the worship of Amma's holy feet) with chanting of mantras which filled the devotees' hearts with a rare bliss. After pada puja, the devotees came one by one to Amma, offered their pranams at Her holy feet and received the prasad. This was followed by the chanting of Lalita Sahasranama – thousand names of the Divine Mother– with offering of flowers at Her divine feet. After the distribution of clothes to the villagers, lunch was served to them. In the afternoon, during the public meeting, the inspiring speeches held the audience spellbound. At night, cultural programmes including 'Kathakali' entertained one and all. Amma's divine presence and the various programmes on the day filled me with blissful gratitude.

Right from the beginning, Amma used to send down refreshing rain showers before Her birthday. The heavy downpour made the atmosphere cool and reduced the hardness of the backwaters where most of the devotees used to take a bath on Her birthday. Amma Herself volunteered to channelize the accumulated rainwater to keep the ashram courtyard dry during the birthday. In those early days, Amma gave rava laddoos (sweet semolina balls) prepared in the ashram as prasad. On one occasion, many days after the birthday celebrations were over, I happened to see that bags full of rava had been left behind in the storeroom. The ashramites in charge of the kitchen and the storeroom were apparently unaware of it. One day, when my medical duties were over, I brought the rava out of the storeroom and spread it in the sun. When it was dry and fresh, I returned it to the storeroom. I was glad that I could save it from getting spoiled. Soon I was called to go to the clinic to give some medicine to Pattiamma, an ashram resident. After dispensing the medicine to her, I spent some time in the clinic with Pattiamma who praised me for saving the rava and blamed the kitchen staff for their carelessness. While I was listening to her lavish praises I heard that Amma was calling me to the kitchen area. Immediately I rushed to Her. Some grains of rava which had fallen from the bags were scattered around in the kitchen yard. The 'careless' kitchen staff also were standing there. To teach them a lesson and to remove traces of vanity and egoism in me, Amma scolded me severely on that day.

On another occasion, Amma scolded me and clarified the reason for that. Once during the initial days, a few senior brahmacharis had come back to the ashram late at night after a spiritual tour. They had brought with them priceless ancient books which they left on the veranda near the Kalari (old temple), before going to sleep. The next morning, they forgot to pick them up on time since they were busily engaged in the morning routine. One middle-aged woman who was staying in the ashram for a short while for some personal reasons, saw those old-looking books on the veranda and sold them along with other articles to be disposed of. I chanced to pass by the veranda without knowing what was going on and she requested me to help her with the calculation. Since she was illiterate, I agreed to help her. Later, when the Swamis looked for their books, she realised the seriousness of her mistake and put the entire blame on me. Amma called me and punished me severely as if I were the culprit. After a while, when Amma saw me in tears, She consoled me saying, "My child, Amma knows very well that you are innocent but Amma can punish none but you." However, by Amma's grace, the next day those valuable books were recovered and brought to the ashram. Amma could never tolerate wastage of food, water, etc. In the early period, She used to come at night to inspect the kitchen, the waste basket, etc. and point out the mistakes of the kitchen staff. One day, while I was walking along the front yard of the ashram with Amma, I happened to spit on the ground. A little of the spittle fell on a leaf of a plant. Amma, the Universal Mother, immediately asked me to clean the leaf. Once I brought food that I had cooked myself, wrapped in a banana leaf from the Haripad branch ashram and offered it to Amma. She ate the offered food, fulfilling my prayer, but pointing to the large leaf I had used, She told me, "My daughter, you should have used a smaller one." I realised my mistake and prayed for forgiveness telling Her, "Amma, I shall keep this leaf as your prasad to remind me of this lesson."

On one of Her birthdays Amma gave me another valuable experience and made me conscious of the fact that She witnesses all the activities of Her children[14]. I spent the whole day taking part in various activities connected with the birthday. Late at night, I waited near Amma's room to have a glimpse of Her when She came back after the Bhava darshan was over. Amma graciously allowed me to be in Her holy company in Her room. When She was about to have Her dinner She told me, "Leela mol, soak some rice in water, powder it, prepare 'puttu'[15] and bring it to me." At first I was not able to figure out how I could carry out the unusual order at that odd hour. But in a flash I realised that Amma's words were meant to remind me of the rice-flour brought by a devotee (Sriram's mother). While handing over the powder to me in the morning, she had described the procedure that was used for preparing it. I was surprised to see how Amma repeated her words exactly and was aware of the smallest wish of Her devotee. Moreover, She kept that lady in mind even after giving darshan to so many thousand people. Not only that, She

---

[14] Oṁ Antevāsi-janāśeṣa ceṣṭāpatita dṛṣṭaye namaḥ - Mata Amritanandamayi Ashtottarasatanamavali 93

[15] A cylindrical cake of rice flour and coconut scrapings cooked in steam.

had graciously revealed Her omniscience to me again by reminding me of the rice powder which I had forgotten to take to Her room. I realised that Amma, who never before had wanted to eat 'puttu' in the night, was asking for it to bless both of us. I rushed to my room to take the rice flour and make it ready for cooking. I did not have to make a fire since there were a lot of live pieces of coal in the fire place. With my mind completely absorbed in Amma and mantra-japa, I prepared the 'puttu' and offered it to Her. She who relishes the loving offering of Her devotees delightfully ate the 'puttu' blessing both of us[16].

The venue for the 50th birthday celebrations of Amma (Amritavarsham 50) was Kochi international stadium. Early morning on September 24th, 2003, I started from Haripad with an intense yearning to have Amma's darshan. While I walked towards Her room, I doubted whether it was proper for me to disturb Her when lakhs and lakhs of people awaited Her presence on the stage. But to my great surprise, I got a glimpse of

---

[16] Oṁ Saprīti-bhukta-bhaktaughanyarpita-sneha-sarpiṣe Namaḥ. – Mata Amritanandamayi Ashtottara Sata Namavali - 97

Amma – the ocean of love and compassion. She was sitting alone in Her room with the door half open as if She were waiting for this little child of Hers. The very next moment I was inside Her room offering my most humble pranams at Her lotus feet. I could converse with Her for a while – it was far beyond my expectation and I was filled with an ineffable joy. In the International stadium, the birthday celebrations started from 24th September and extended for four days. The first day was dedicated to equality of religions, 2nd for women's empowerment, 3rd for the youth and 4th which was Amma's birthday was for world peace and the upliftment of the poor and downtrodden. 191 nations which were members of the UNO participated in the unique celebrations. The message given by Amma on the first day was, "The essence of all religions is love. Love is the only religion. The idea that only one religion must exist and others must perish is not a sign of progress, but barbarianism. Each religion has its own path. All religions should march forward in unity and work for the well being of the whole world." After many special programmes in Amma's inspiring presence, She started giving darshan from midnight onwards. The second and third day of the celebrations were also special with many excellent programmes. The fourth day - September 27 - was Amma's birthday. Amma, adorned in dazzling white garments sat on the stage with a divine smile. Lakhs of people had assembled to have the vision of the Universal Mother. Swami Amritaswarupanandaji did the Padaabhisheka and the Archana with the offering of lotus petals. The notes of the mantra "*Om Amṛteśvaryai Namaḥ*" reverberated everywhere. Amma, immersed in samadhi, received the love and devotion of Her children. "May this big gathering bring peace and hope to those who are immersed in misery and sorrow. Amma is more concerned with the cleaning of Her children's minds than the pada-pooja for Her. Nowadays we have equipments to clean the exterior, removing even the most minute particles of dust and dirt, but we fail to remove false pride and egoism from our mind"- Amma's divine exhortation got imprinted in the devotee's minds. Amma advised that Her children who make adventurous trips to the sea and space should also dive deep into their minds and discover the mysteries there-in. By 11 a.m. the public meeting started in Amma's divine presence with distribution of awards and gold medals, and inauguration of many humanitarian activities. At night, Amma was giving darshan to thousands of Her children, wiping their tears and bestowing peace and solace on them. Meanwhile, many soul stirring cultural programmes went on side by side on the stage. Amma's darshan continued upto 9 o'clock in the morning next day. Thus Amma, the Universal Mother, imparted the fragrance of selflessness and divine love to the golden celebrations of Amritavarsham - 50.

Right from the beginning of my ashram life Amma enabled me to experience that She is the omniscient indwelling Self who directs my mind, body and intellect. One morning, during the first monsoon of my ashram life, Amma called me to Her. She was sitting on the veranda of one of the huts, repairing its door. I found that all my personal belongings were lying in the slushy front yard. Amma continued to work on the door ignoring me completely. I sat at Her lotus feet on the ground. When Amma finished Her work, She got up and went away. I was happy that I could sit with Amma. I guessed that She must have thrown my clothes and other belongings out of the hut deliberately to free me of the sense of 'I' and 'mine'. I had abandoned the thoughts of "my house, relatives, friends, job, etc." when I had joined the ashram. The feeling of 'my things,' Amma was kindly taking away. Though I felt rather reluctant to take the things back into the hut initially, later I also joined the other ashramites in collecting them. While washing away the dirt from the saris, I mentally repeated:

"Entinenikkini vesham?
Amma ente sowbhagya vishesham"

("Amma, beautiful garments I don't need. You are the bestower of all that I need" —improvised from the song 'Ningalil Aranumunto')

In the evening I followed Amma to the seashore to meditate and I tried to concentrate on the Divine Mother as the infinite ocean of bliss. Amma got up after meditation and walked along the seashore. The waves gently touched Her sacred feet to purify themselves and Amma sang the bhajans, "You are creation and creator," "Anandamayi Brahmamayi", etc. After sunset, Amma came back to the ashram and started the evening bhajans. After a few songs, She started singing "Ningalil Aranumunto." I felt as if the bhajan was specially meant for me when She sang the line —

"Entinenikkini vesham?"

I wept with joy, feeling Amma's omniscience, love and kindness.

On a later occasion, when Amma was on a Western tour, I was sitting and meditating in a hut, after which I sat for a while gazing at the sky. It was monsoon season and the sky had a unique appearance with huge dark clouds, interspersed with bits of white glittering in the morning sun. My mind was transported to a higher realm and I was inspired to compose a poem in Malayalam.

Once I was waiting on the way side,
Yearning to have a glimpse of Amma.
Humming a sweet melody,
Stepping daintily on the pebbled floor,
A small stream was gurgling by.
The greenery, trees and plants
Were swaying in the breeze,
Murmuring the sweet divine syllable "Amma".
The birds flying high in the sky were singing,

> "O Amma, O Amma."
> *Amma's sparkling eyes and*
> *Her divine gaze I saw in the sky,*
> *While I was lost in the inspiring nature.*
> *The sea of spiritual emotions surged in me,*
> *And I heard Amma's words,*
> *O my children,*
> *You are verily the embodiment of love,*
> *Try to be loving to all,*
> *Lead a life full of love and light.*
> *Realize your true nature,*
> *Be free from sorrows and delusion.*

I used to sit contemplating on that poem on the veranda of the hut during evenings when the setting sun poured out dazzling colours in the sky. Occasionally one brahmacharini also joined me, listening to the poem in Malayalam. Soon after Amma gave me this poetic experience, we were fortunate to read a letter from Amma.[17] She had written, "My Children, don't be sad thinking that no one loves you. Always contemplate that you are the embodiments of Love and learn to love

---

[17] In those days Amma used to send letters to the ashram when She was on the foreign tours.

one and all." I was overwhelmed to see that the advice Amma had given me internally through the poem was the same as that which was in Her letter. I blissfully experienced that Amma is 'sarvāntaryāmiṇi'[18] – the Divine Mother who directs the inner senses of Her children. The brahmacharini who was a direct witness to that experience was also delighted. I offered that poem 'The Vision' mentally at Amma's holy feet and it was soon published in the Malayalam Matruvani.

Once Amma was travelling to Thalassery, a city in northern Kerala for performing the prana-pratishtha (installation ceremony) in the Brahmasthanam temple there. I proceeded from Kunnamkulam (a town in Thrissur district) after a spiritual programme there with a few devotees, desirous of following Amma. After a while, She graciously sent a car to take me to Her and allowed me to travel with Her. In Thalassery, on the first day of the installation festival, I was with Amma in Her room waiting to serve Her. After giving darshan to a few devotees in the room, She was discussing some urgent ashram matters

---

[18] Sri Lalitasahasranama 819

on the phone. I was keeping Amma's clothes, etc. ready for Her to use. Then I found that Her hairband was missing. I thought I would go out and ask brahmacharini Lakshmi about it. Then I heard that one more person was coming soon for Amma's darshan and I was in a dilemma as to what to do next. Amma, who was talking on the phone at the other end of the room, pointed towards the bathroom. As soon as I went inside the bathroom I was wonderstruck to see Her hairband there. Once more I was convinced that Amma who is all knowing fulfils even the smallest needs of Her children, even while She is busily engaged in various activities. On the next day when Amma gave me the opportunity to address the audience, I shared that experience also with them.

On another occasion, Amma was coming back with Her children to the ashram after the North Indian tour. When we reached Kozhikode, it was time for lunch. As directed by Amma, all buses were diverted to the university campus there. When we reached the campus, She asked all the buses to stop in the premises of some residential quarters. She alighted from Her car and started walking towards one house. Seeing Amma, the man of the house came running to Her. He who was a professor in the university welcomed Amma to his house. He was shedding tears of joy and none of us knew what was happening. The professor made arrangements for Her to sit and have Her lunch there. He showed the ashramites also a suitable place to sit and take their food. Since I was with Amma in his house, I understood what was happening. Though the professor and his family were devoted to Amma, they had not had an opportunity to get Her darshan. When Amma had been in Bangalore (Bengaluru), his wife and children participated in Her programme there and had Her darshan. When the professor came to know about it, his yearning to see Amma became all the more intense. Amma, the Universal Mother, went to him and blessed him fulfilling his wish. A similar incident occurred while Amma was returning from Mumbai with the ashramites. Soon after the journey started, Her car which was running perfectly in good condition stopped suddenly. The owner of an automobile workshop nearby saw Her and came running to Her. There again

Amma was fulfilling his long cherished desire, because mysteriously Her car became functional again without any repair.

Amma has saved many from the clutches of alchohol addiction and Suresh was one among them. Addicted as he was to alcohol, he grew indifferent to his duties both in his office and at home. Not only did he refuse to go to office but he also took away his wife's salary for buying hard drinks. The family members tried to bring him back to normalcy but in vain. They were totally disgusted with him. Once, his wife Sarala came to me in despair and complained about him while I was in the Thrissur branch. Since the construction of the ashram building had not been finished, I had to stay with Ramaniamma, a close devotee of Amma. Sarala who was in tears told me about her miserable life and requested me to visit their house and pray for them. She explained to me that Suresh was reluctant to face anyone because of his inferiority complex. She appealed to me that I should reach as early as possible in the morning before Suresh left the house. Ramaniamma and I went to Sarala's house the next morning. Somehow Suresh had known about our visit and sneaked away. Yet Sarala hopefully welcomed us and arranged for the pooja. Suresh's father soliloquised, "Many prayers and poojas have been already done without any benefit. Why should we conduct another pooja today?" "Let us have faith in Amma and pray again and hope for the best", I encouraged him. The family members eagerly participated in the short pooja and archana, chanting the 108 names of Amma, offering flowers. I specially prayed with them, "O Divine Mother, bestow on us peace and prosperity and make our prayers fruitful. You are the sole refuge for us. Kindly save your children from misery and sorrow." I instructed them to keep the offered flowers in the pooja room and to pray continuously. We waited for a while for Suresh but he did not turn up. Suddenly, by Amma's grace, an idea flashed in my mind and accordingly I left a small note for Suresh with Sarala. The note written by Ramaniamma had two sentences – "Tapasyamrita is in charge of the Idukki ashram branch and needs your help. Please come to our house as soon as possible." Tapasyamrita Chaitanya, one of the senior brahmacharis of Amma and son of Ramaniamma, was known to Suresh. We prayed to Amma who is the ocean of compassion to make our attempt successful, and took leave of Sarala and the family members. It was really amazing that Amma graciously granted our prayers. Suresh, after reading the note, soon stopped drinking and came to Ramaniamma's house, ready to go to Idukki. She happily handed over certain articles which would be useful in Idukki, and picking them up he took leave of us. In Idukki, he participated in service oriented activities and abandoned his old habit of drinking. Eventually, he and his family became Amma's devotees and led a happy and peaceful life.

Amma gave me an experience revealing the import of Her statement that temples are centres of sadhana and the idol in the temple, like a mirror, helps one to cleanse the mind by facilitating easy perception of God. There are people who misconstrue temple worship saying that idols are nothing but stone and wood. Swami Vivekananda replies to them that none of the temple worshippers ever pray, "O stone, save me" or "O wood, save me," instead, all experience the presence of God in the idol and pray, "Save me O God," which means that they see God in both the stone and wooden images. Once during the early days, Amma was returning from the West. In those days, the ashramites, including the brahmacharinis, used to go to the airport to see Amma's arrival and to be with Her while She travelled to the ashram in the ashram vehicle. In the airport all were eagerly waiting to see Her. I saw that all were running to a spot saying, "Amma has come." I also joined them so that I too could see Her there but all that I could see there was a glass door. I was disappointed. But very soon I understood that through the glass door I could see Amma climbing down from the plane. I was very happy to see Her and in a flash She revealed to me the efficacy of idol worship through the example of the glass door. I felt that just as Amma could be seen through the glass door, God could also be easily perceived in the idol.

Amma gave me another blissful experience during one programme in the Sri Rama temple, Triprayar (Thrissur district). A temporary stall of Amma's ashram branch used to function in the temple premises during the Ekadasi festival.[19]

---

[19] 11th day of the lunar cycle, an important day for seekers since it is considered to be the birthday of Maha Vishnu

Once I was invited to the temple to conduct a spiritual programme there during the festival. Dr Nalini, a close devotee of Amma, took the initiative to organise the programme. As the day of the programme was nearing, one of the associates of the ashram branch raised an opposition to the programme and told me, "Swamini amma, you must cancel the programme because the temple authorities will not allow the chanting of the 108 names of Amma. Most of us are also against it." When Dr. Nalini came to know about the opposition, she was very upset and said, "All the arrangements for the programme have been made. Please don't cancel it." It was for the first time that the temple authorities had come forward to organise a programme in Amma's name. It came to my mind that Amma would be displeased if we cancel the programme at the last minute. Since the programme was in the Sri Rama temple, I thought that I could very well chant the hymn of 108 names of Sri Rama. Dr. Nalini was very happy on hearing this. I was very familiar with the hymn since I used to chant it often. The opposition party did not like the idea and asked me, "How can you chant names of Sri Rama in Amma's programme? Is it not an injustice to Amma and Her organisation?" I again tried to convince them saying, "Amma and Sri Rama are one and the same. She will be pleased with the hymn of Sri Rama." But they retorted, "Can you show us that Amma and Sri Rama are one?" "Certainly, by Amma's grace, I will be able to do so," I answered them.

In the afternoon, on the day of our programme, the bhajan troop arrived and we rehearsed the hymn beginning with "Suddha Brahma Paratpara Rama" from the "Bhajanamritam" to the accompaniment of the harmonium and other musical instruments. In the evening I started the programme with a speech on Amma's life and temple worship, followed by the hymn and Amma's bhajans. After a few bhajans, I started one bhajan on Amma, "Devi Devi Devi Amriteshwari" and to our great surprise we saw that the replica of the idol in the temple was brought out of the sanctum sanctorum to the entrance of the stage in a spectacular procession, exactly at that moment. The entire audience, including the pilgrims to the Sabarimala temple, were thrown into a rapture and paid their homage to the deity. It could only have been Amma's unparalleled grace that made the two events — the beginning of Amma's bhajan and the starting of the procession coincide in this manner. It was clear to me and the audience that Amma was showing Her oneness with the deity. That revelation of Amma filled my mind with a rare bliss. Amma was disclosing to all those who participated in the programme, including me, the import of the Vedic mantra - *"Ekam sat viprah bahudhā vadanti"* (Rig Veda 2/3/22) - Truth is one, the great ones call it by many names.

In Sanatana Dharma the One Truth has many expressions enabling seekers to grasp it easily. Each one can choose the path that leads him to the goal. This doctrine of 'Ishta devata' — the beloved deity, is special only to Hinduism. It is the duty of the seekers to stick to the path they have adopted. Amma advises Her children to defy those fanatics who destroy the faith of others by imposing their own ideas, and to follow the spiritual teachers who show the right path. It is very essential to learn scriptural truths from a spiritual teacher. Amma reminds us that at present, academic education aims at making one capable of earning money, whereas in the past it imparted eternal values also. Amma has founded many institutions for imparting the eternal wisdom of which She Herself is the example. The Hindu scriptures include 18 different sections of knowledge, namely four Vedas, six Vedangas, Mimansas, Nyayashastra, Purnanam, Dharmashastra, Ayurveda, Dhanurveda, Gandharvaveda and Arthaveda. It is the duty of the Hindus to imbibe the messages of the scriptures, live accordingly and spread them in society at large. Amma says that it is the only way to rise above the fanatic approach of propagandists of other religions who appear with their inane arguments anywhere and everywhere — at bus stops, railway stations, in buses and trains and also in houses. Once I met such a person on a train while I was returning to Amritapuri after a programme at the University in Ettimadai. I had been invited to the Amrita Vishwa Vidyapeetham (university campus) in Ettimadai to address the first year engineering students. As I was walking to the stage along with the professors, students started to clap their hands. The Head of the Department was irritated and asked them to stop. But they did not listen to him. Somehow I began my speech suggesting that it would be more enjoyable if they chant '*Oṁ Namaḥ Śivāya*' while clapping. They liked it and started to do so. After a while they also responded positively to my next suggestion, i.e. to chant the mantra '*Om Amṛteśvaryai Namaḥ*' also. Soon they stopped clapping and diverted their attention to my speech and then to the guided meditation chanting the pranava mantra 'OM'. The students appeared to enjoy the meditation and for quite some time they sat immersed in it and pindrop silence prevailed in the hall. When it was time to conclude the programme, I had to wake them up, chanting the Omkara mantra. On the next day, I was returning to Amritapuri with a few of the ashramites in the train. One man who was in the next seat started to talk to one of us. Slowly he started questioning her faith in Amma. He argued that none but Christ is real and raised wrong arguments to defeat her. Then he tried to object to the 'advaita' philosophy by asking, "How can a doctor, school teacher and the housewife be the same?" Then the nectarine words of Amma came to our rescue. I told him, "The fridge, fan and electric bulb may look different outwardly, but the electricity that makes them function is one and the same. Similarly, the doctor, the teacher and the housewife may seem to be different personalities, but the life force in them is the same. In deep sleep when thoughts and other modifications disappear, they remain in their true Self and all the differences vanish. We have experienced that Amma who always revels in the atman – the pure Consciousnes, is beyond mind, body and intellect. She manifests Godly qualities like truth, love, mercy and patience, setting an example to mankind. Amma sees God in all that exists and awakens everyone by Her loving address, "My darling child, the essence of OM." She does not address anyone as a sinner. We worship Amma in order to realize Her as the indwelling Self in all beings. One who knows God as all pervading Consciousness – the parabrahman – verily becomes God.

> 'Sa yo ha vai tatparamaṁ brahmaveda
> brahmaiva bhavati[20]'

Hearing me, he stopped his arguments and sat quietly for the rest of the journey.

---

[20] Mundakopanishad - 3,2,9

Amma who is the Universal Mother exhorts us to protect religion and culture at any cost which in turn leads us to the supreme goal. May Amma bless us to imbibe Her teachings and make them part and parcel of our life and attain liberation. Amma, I prostrate at your sacred feet again and again with an intense desire to join you eternally.

Oṁ Namaḥ Śivāya

www.ingramcontent.com/pod-product-compliance
Lightning Source LLC
Chambersburg PA
CBHW070617050426
42450CB00011B/3074